The Science of Dreaming

Contents

SCHOLASTIC

Published in the UK by
Scholastic Education, 2024
Scholastic Distribution Centre, Bosworth Avenue,
Tournament Fields, Warwick, CV34 6UQ
Scholastic Ireland, 89E Lagan Road, Dublin
Industrial Estate, Glasnevin, Dublin, D11 HP5F

1 2 3 4 5 6 7 8 9   4 5 6 7 8 9 0 1 2 3

Printed by Ashford Colour Press

This book is made of materials from
well-managed, FSC®-certified forests
and other controlled sources.

MIX
Paper from
responsible sources
FSC   FSC® C011748
www.fsc.org

A CIP catalogue record for this book is available
from the British Library.

ISBN 978-0702-32733-9

Author
Jonny Walker

Editorial team
Rachel Morgan, Vicki Yates, Alison Gilbert,
Jennie Clifford

Design team
Dipa Mistry, Andrea Lewis and We Are Grace

Photographs
p4–5 fizkes/Shutterstock
p6–7 Orla/iStock
p7 (man) Prostock-studio/Shutterstock
p8, p24 (background) Improviser/Shutterstock
p9 xxxstudio/Shutterstock
p10–11 Roman Zaiets/Shutterstock
p11 (brain) SpeedKingz/Shutterstock
p12 0nemylove/Shutterstock
p13 (brain scan) My Portfolio/Shutterstock
p14 Elena Ray/Shutterstock
p15 Opat Suvi/Shutterstock
p16–17 SeventyFour/Shutterstock
p18–19 Macrovector/Shutterstock
p20 agsandrew/Shutterstock
p21 Pixel-Shot/Shutterstock
p22 Danii Brown Photography/Shutterstock

Illustrations
Cover Matthew Taylor Wilson/The Bright Agency
p4 (star icons) Victoria Morozova/Shutterstock
p8 (woman) Rumka vodki/Shutterstock
p13, 14, 21 (icons) Skylines/Shutterstock
p13, 14, 21 (icons) kuroksta/Shutterstock
p17 (music icons) proksima/iStock
p23 (leg) afry_harvy/Shutterstock
p23 (spider) KR image/Shutterstock

How to use this book

This book practises these letters and letter sounds:

are (as in 'rare')	ture (as in 'pictures')
a (as in 'recall')	a (as in 'what')
ear (as in 'learn')	sc (as in 'scientists')
ch (as in 'technology')	

Here are some of the words in the book that use the sounds above:

architecture nightmares science fall

This book uses these common tricky words:

are to because they our do of the through eyes thoughts people many their into

Before reading

- Read the title and look at the cover. Discuss what this book might be about.

During reading

- If necessary, sound it out and then blend the sounds to read the word: e-x-i-s-t, exist.
- Pause every so often to talk about the information.

After reading

- Talk about what has been read.
- Use the index on page 24 to select any pages to revisit.

Dreams are fascinating. Dreams exist, but it is challenging to study them because they happen in our minds.

What do scientists understand about dreams?

What are Dreams?

Dreams are imaginary stories, pictures and events we think of whilst asleep.

Everybody has a 'sleep architecture'. This means the pattern of sleep we go through.

Sleep Architecture

Stage **1** Falling asleep

Stage **2** Light sleep

Stage **3** Deep sleep

Stage **4** Dream sleep

In dream sleep our muscles relax but our eyes dart about. Researchers believe our eyes are 'seeing' our dream-scenes.

Scientific technology can capture and analyse brain activity.

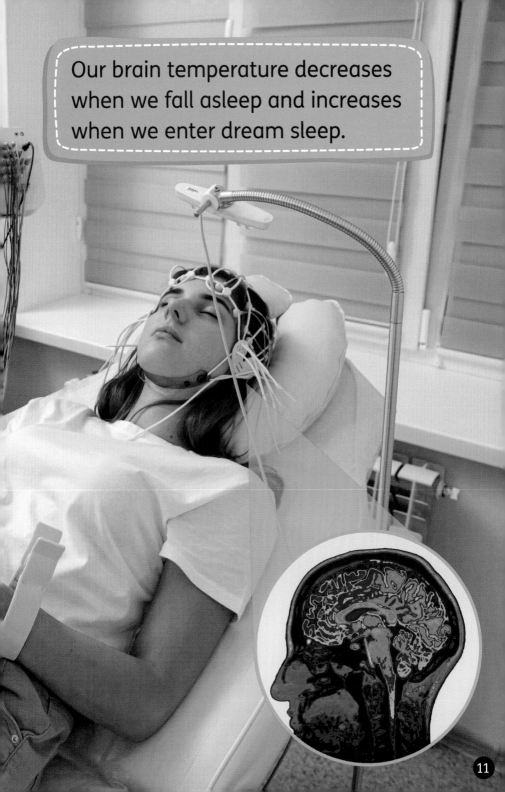

Our brain temperature decreases when we fall asleep and increases when we enter dream sleep.

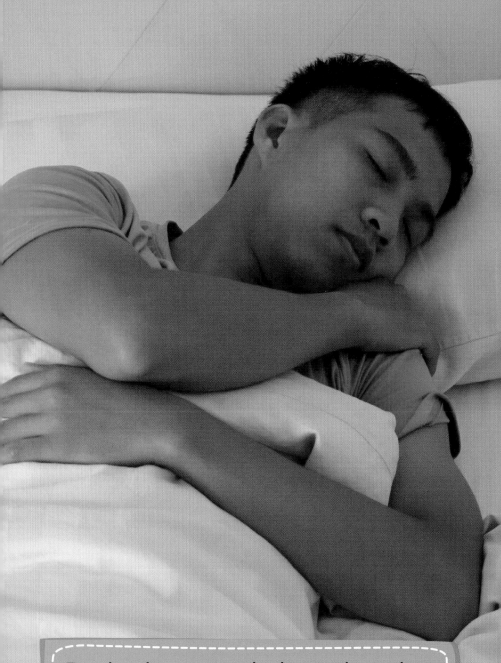

Fascinating research shows that when we sleep, the brain cleans itself.

A liquid washes through our brains and pushes out toxic chemicals that pollute it.
We are literally brainwashed.

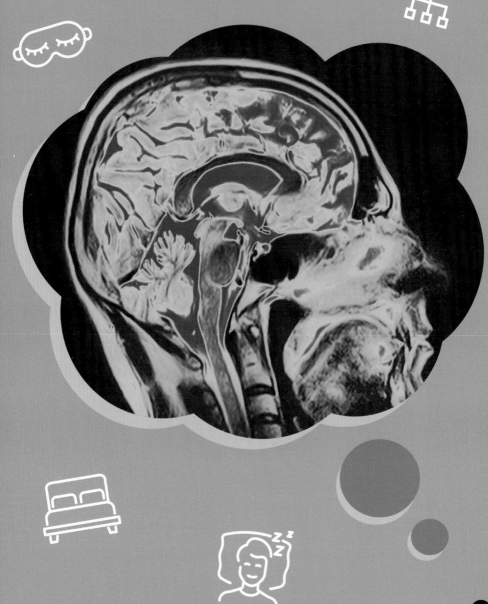

Dreaming

There might be memories and thoughts mixed up with fantasy in our dreams.

We may recall some dreams.
Most are forgotten by the morning.

Dreams have always fascinated people. Many artists are inspired by dreaming.

Songwriters, such as Taylor Swift, have written songs inspired by dreams.

Nightmares feel worse than dreams. Nightmares can haunt our sleep. Some authors of horror tales found their monsters in their nightmares.

We don't fully understand the mind. We cannot explain why our brains pull us into nightmare scenes that scare us.

In a rare sort of dream, dreamers recognise they are dreaming and can choose what happens.

Some people walk and talk in their sleep.
Sleepwalking happens in deep sleep,
not dream sleep.

Early research into animals' sleep shows that they could be dreamers too.

They seem to have similar sleep architecture to humans.

What would dogs dream of?
Do spiders have nightmares?

Researchers still have lots to learn about the science of dreaming.

Index